SEEKING YOU

Seeking You
Poems by Jeong Ho-seung
Translated by Brother Anthony of Taizé

Copyright © October 01, 2025 Jeong Ho-seung (original poems), Brother Anthony (translations)

No part of this book may be used or performed without written consent of the author, if living, except for critical articles or reviews.'

Seeking You
Copyright © Jeong Ho-seung
All rights reserved.

Originally published in Korea by Changbi Publishers, Inc.
English Translation copyright © 2024 by Brother Anthony
English edition is published by Trio House Press in arrangement with Changbi Publishers, Inc.

This book is published with the support of the Literature Translation Institute of Korea (LTI Korea).

ISBN: 978-1-949487-51-0
LCCN: 2025939368

Interior design by Natasha Kane
Cover design by Joel W. Coggins
Translation by Brother Anthony of Taizé

Trio House Press, Inc.
Minneapolis
www.triohousepress.org

Table of Contents

Part 1

Bird Droppings 1	3
Branded	4
Bird Droppings 2	5
Bird Droppings 3	6
Latrine	7
A Snowy Path	8
Dog Shit	9
A Shovel	10
Becoming a Monk	11
Hell is Heaven	12
A Snowman	13
My Heart	14
Winter Lotus Pond	15
Drinking the Water that Birds Drink	16
Red Bird	17
A Broom	18
Eye Drops	19
Seeking You	20
A Mud Chair	21
An Evening Spent Thinking of Shadows	22
I Long to see a Chimney	23
Self-Introduction	24
Yet Another Regret	25
A Poem Written by Birds as Footprints on the First Snow	26
By the Window	27

Part 2

Immortality	31
For Peonies	32
The Snowman's Grave	33
Silence	34
I Kneel	35

A Snail	36
Raising Birds	37
Stumbling Block	38
Dreaming Dust	39
The Road to Buseoksa Temple	40
To Become an Empty Bowl	41
A Salmon	42
Looking at a White Pine	43
Arirang, Even if Trampled On	44
Today's Resolution	45
For the Last Time	46
Concerning that Loneliness	47
To a Flock of Teal	48
At Bulguksa Temple	49
To a Wooden Fish	50
At the Racetrack	51
Photos Taken by Someone Blind	52
A Black Mask	53
Sad and Happy	54
Sungnye-mun, Seoul's South Gate	55

Part 3

An Ant	59
Autobiography	60
You	61
My Heartless Heart	62
When I First Held Your Hand	63
While Flowers Fade	64
To Kasyapa	65
A Trap	66
A Fire	67
Stumbling	68
A Gate Crasher	69
Off the Train	70
Turn into Charcoal	71
A Pile of Ash	72
Drenched in Dew	73

A Blade of Grass	74
In Order to Become Mud	75
Crossing a River Alone	76
Evening with Swords	77
To the Woodpecker	78
Your Sword	79
A Melancholy Officetel	80
To my Demon	81
To a Winter River	82

Part 4

Morning Star	85
Star Rice	86
Piercing Your Heart	87
To Love	88
Yearned-for Yearning	89
Candlelight	90
Food	91
Mokpo Station	92
A Thimble	93
Longed-for Lamplight	94
Commemorative Photo	95
Leading my Shadow	96
House of Tears	97
Birds' Shadows Do Not Fly	98
Inside the Word 'Whale' There Is Mother	99
Homecoming	100
Break-Up	101
By the Seomjin River	102
Ginkgo Leaves	103
The Road along the Wall of Deoksugung	104
A Night in Silla	105
Rags	106
Pyeongchang-dong Monastery	107
In Gwanghwamun	108
Boundary	109

Part 5

Prison in Heaven	113
Indulgence	114
After Reusrrection	115
Old Clothes	116
A Bus Stop	117
Every Time I Look at the Clock	118
The Last Bus	119
To Time	120
The Last Moment	121
In a Delta	122
When Evening Comes	123
The Fragrance of Tears	124
Poison	125
To Judas	126
Judas' Last Testament	127
Evening Meeting with Judas	128
A Miracle	129
Before a Confessional	130
Guide to Confession	131
Prayer of Haemi-eupseong Pagoda Tree	132
Wounds	133
Entering Nirvana	134
So, Farewell Now	135
Funeral Mass	136
Low Tide	137
Transforming our Minds, the Miracle of Poverty	139
Poet's Note, 2020	149
Acknowledgments	151
About the Author	153
About the Translator	155

Part 1

Bird Droppings 1

Bird droppings got into my eyes.
For the first time in my life
I washed my eyes clean with bird droppings.
That stopped me seeing the human landscape
that I thought I wanted to see
but did not really need to see.
Thank you.

Branded

I was branded,
not as a human, but as a beast,
a human being worse than a beast.
Not so.
I branded myself,
not as a human, but as a bird,
a little bird
flying across the blue winter sky
on its way to visit the Buddha.

Bird Droppings 2

When I see bird droppings on the ground
as I walk along,
it makes me feel relieved.
Since among human paths there's a beautiful path
where birds leave their droppings,
by walking along that path
today I become a beautiful human being.

Bird Droppings 3

I give all my food to the birds
while I just peck at the birds' feed.
Walking along a pathless path,
no matter how hungry I am
I give the birds all my food
while I peck at the birds' feed all my life long.
After a bird has enjoyed my food
it shits while flying far up in the sky.
Its droppings fall to the ground.
Birds do not shit in the sky,
ultimately they shit on the ground.
Before you can say that a human path is beautiful
there has to be bird shit on it
and I have to walk along that path
if I am to become beautiful.

Latrine

I am your latrine.
Whether it's a rainy day
or a snowy day
or a day when tears fall
and dead leaves fall,
any time,
leave your shit in my breast
and go in peace.

A Snowy Path

Laughing,
I walk along a snowy path.
Leaving myself behind,
simply laughing,
leaving my dead mother behind,
leaving behind even the wife who left me,
not being stupid,
like a necessary fool,
laughing gaily,
leaving the path,
I fall.

Dog Shit

A pile of dog shit sits
quietly cross-legged
on the street.
The wind is quiet, too.
I sit down cross-legged
beside the dog shit
and gaze at the distant mountain.
If the mountain doesn't come to me,
I can go to the mountain.
A worker ant
busily
dragging a large leaf
passes beside the dog shit.

A Shovel

A shovel is resting,
leaning against a persimmon tree.
After doing a lifetime's work
the shovel is quiet now.

After rising at dawn,
digging trenches to let water flow onto rice fields,
scooping up dog shit
lying coiled in the middle of the yard,

Since Father died,
the shovel
Father always carried about with him
has been resting in silence, peacefully.

As it slowly rusts in the rain and wind,
perhaps not expecting anyone to come,
perhaps not even wanting to see Father,
it smiles in the sunshine.

Becoming a Monk

Snow falls heavily on winter fields.
One tiny bird comes flying from somewhere
and perches quietly on an electricity pylon
resembling the pagoda at Bulguksa Temple.
The pylon turns into a bird and spreads silent wings.
The wind blows,
more heavy snow falls, and as the bird,
after sitting on the pylon, silently flies off through the falling snow,
the pylon turns into a bird and flies away too.
Are you on your way to become a monk
in some mountain temple where snow is falling?

Hell is Heaven

Hell is heaven.
Hell, too, has its flower beds,
rain falls high up in the mountains,
birds fly,
there is love even in Hell

Even if no one takes me there
while I live in this world,
I will surely go to visit Hell one day.

Even if I'm kicked out of Hell
I'll come back again,
meet you,
love you.

A Snowman

The snowman's head had been sent rolling off like a Buddha's head.
No one saw who did it.
The apartment security guard claimed he had been guarding the
    snowman all night,
but somebody cut off the snowman's head,
someone who hates people killed the snowman instead.
The snowman died on my behalf.
The snowman remained standing there with his head cut off
until I came back from work in the evening.
I felt as if my severed head was rolling about
so I quickly rolled a snowball to repair the snowman.
Just then the snowman picked up his severed head with both hands
and slowly started off along the snowy path where the snow had
    stopped falling.

My Heart

Every time I throw out the trash
my heart is in the trash bag.
Still alive,
jumping and leaping,
enclosed in a standard green trash bag,
my heart is crying.
Don't cry.
If you keep on crying, you'll upset me.
Even if I clench my fists and open my eyes wide like a father,
my heart stays crouching like a child.
Sometimes, as if comforting a crying child,
I take my heart out of the trash bag,
carry it back home, wash it clean,
and put it next to the crucifix.
A few days later,
when I leave the house to throw out the trash,
my heart is back in the trash bag again.
My heart is trash now,
the heart of my loving.

Winter Lotus Pond

This is the hospice ward,
the funeral home that sent you off,
the ruined temple where I went with your youth
that winter beneath a clear sky,
the vault of truth where you are interred,
the beautiful tomb of lotuses.
Backs bent above frozen water,
the fine bones of lotuses still burning,
the calligraphed wills written by the mass of lotuses,
each in mysterious hieroglyphs
which if deciphered, yield the words of the Avatamsaka Sutra.
After sending you off like froth,
I go fluttering here and there as sleet
while beneath the ice covering the frozen winter lotus pond,
today again, the fish are performing a hundred and eight prostrations
as they forgive me for wasting my life and collapsing.

Drinking the Water that Birds Drink

There is always some water left
in the plastic goblet on the old table that my wife made
on the veranda of our first floor apartment,
even if the birds regularly fly in to drink the water.
Sometimes there is bird shit in the water
so that at first, I kept throwing the water away
but nowadays I drink it
since the birds have left it for me.
I tried to drink only flowing river water,
but couldn't even drink the water
that lay stagnant on the pebbles by the river's edge.
I preferred, when thirsty, to drink a desert,
or climb up a cliff and drink salt water.
I was thirsty throughout my life,
even my tears dried up,
and today, I drink the water that birds drink
since they have left it for me,
thirsty no matter how much I drink and drink,
now as I am dying.

.

Red Bird

Birds come flying
and peck at my heart, that I left on the old table.
They refuse to eat it, saying that the heart of my youth,
which I tried to give back to my mother before she died,
contains deadly poison.
Birds come flying and peck,
saying there is a poison of detoxification in my aged heart.
Just as they peck at the last persimmon
hanging alone on a high branch,
birds peck at my heart then go flying off through the winter sky.
Finally unable to give back to my mother
the heart that I should give back,
I become a red bird and disappear.

A Broom

A mountainside temple in winter.
Once all the snow piled in the courtyard
has been swept away,
the broom is quiet like a Buddha,
leaning on a pine tree
at the side of the path leading to the latrines,
Tits, nuthatches and bulbuls
come flying down to the remote snowfield
and peck at the stubby broom,
hoping for something to eat.
Perching by the broom,
eyes closed,
they are quiet.

Eye Drops

Dip the brush of truth
into the ink of mercy
and apply eye drops
to the eyes of my dark desire.
Let the light of the eye-drops shine.
I longed to look up to You
at least once before leaving
but I haven't yet managed to open my eyes.
I have lived my whole life unable to open my eyes,
let alone the eyes of my heart.
Let me apply eye drops
one last time before I die.
With the lamp of the eye drops brightly shining
I will see You at least once,
cry hard,
then go to Hell forever.

Seeking You

Holding my severed head in both hands,
I walk ahead, gazing at the distant mountains.
I walk towards You,
whom I have longed to meet but could never meet, all my life long.
I advance, then fall,
like saints carrying their severed heads.
It's warm.
Finally, spring has come!
Flowers are blooming once again in the distant mountains,
so where on earth are You?
Are You with the birds that go flying off after pecking at azaleas?
One saint washed the head he was carrying,
cleaning it in a river,
but I collapse and fall asleep forever,
unable even to reach the river's bank.
I've spent my whole life looking for You but couldn't find You,
simply left my head rolling about
on the ground...

A Mud Chair

It's raining
and someone
has brought me a chair made of clay,
telling me to sit on it.
A shower is pouring down.

A chair I have to sit on
although I don't want to.
A mud chair
I will be obliged to sit on
just once, one day.

The shower did not stop,
turned into a downpour,
mud became mud again
and the chair disappeared.

Sitting on the mud chair
like one condemned to death,
thinking of Mother,
I disappeared with the chair.

An Evening Spent Thinking of Shadows

The shadow of a person has never once
become the shadow of a bird.
The shadow of a person has never once
become the shadow of a tree,
or the shadow of a snowman.
But there are times when the shadow of a bird
becomes the shadow of a person
and goes flying off across the blue sky.
There are times when the shadow of a tree
becomes the shadow of a person
and quietly hugs you from behind
when you have lost your mother.
And there are times when the shadow of a snowman
becomes the shadow of a person
and walks slowly with you along a distant alley leading homeward,
holding hands with your mother's shadow.

I Long to See a Chimney

A heart missing someone is like a chimney,
but where have all those chimneys gone?
Where have all those chimneys gone
from which the smoke of rice cooking gently rose
as hungry neighbors, when evening came,
served as one another's rice in the twilight glow?
Families stay frozen in the cold winter breeze,
until the floor where they huddle like silkworms grows warm,
when Mother breaks pine branches and lights the fire in the hearth.
I long to see the chimneys where wrens once sat,
tails raised stiff like eaves,
looming amidst the acrid white smoke.
Today, leaning against a warm chimney
after walking along a back alley of Jongno strewn with briquette ash,
I long to see geese flying north.

Self-Introduction

My ear is a mouth.
My mouth is an ear.
When I get up in the morning and look at my face
my mouth is attached to my ear,
my ear is attached to my mouth.

So I now speak with my ear,
listen with my mouth,
and when I smile, I smile with my ear
and sometimes at the smile of my ear
wild birds perching on pine trees
smile with me.

No matter where I go,
or who I meet,
because I speak with my ear and listen with my mouth,
I keep talking in birdsong
and hear everyone's words
as birdsong.

Yet Another Regret

When I began to love You,
at first I wanted to run to a tree
and say: I love you

At first, I wanted to run to the smallest bird
perched on a tree
and whisper: I love you

So far I've not been able to say
'I love you' to anyone
and I've grown old.
I've become an elderly child.

A Poem Written by Birds as Footprints on the First Snow

I will never come back.
I will never spread my wings and return to the village where humans live,
will never become part of a dirty human landscape.
Though through the first snow cornelian cherries
gently reveal their red breasts and wait for me,
I will never again fly from afar into human hearts
and sing, no matter how long they wait.
Now I will fly to a place where there are no living and no dead,
where there is nowhere to go back to, no time to go back to,
and I will say:
Humans, shut up and be silent.

By the Window

Let nobody's mouth
say with a bird's voice
that the short moment it takes a bird
to fly
from this branch to that branch
is what we call a lifetime.

A bird's voice
can sing with the Buddha
and can make morning offerings,
whereas a human mouth
cannot pray with the Buddha,
nor even share a cup of tea with him.

Part 2

Immortality

Even immortality disappears.
How can there be something that never disappears?
Even immortal tears disappear.
Who will survive and never disappear?
Neither Mother nor you.
That bulbul bird, the red cornelian cherries,
even the distant Pole Star's blue starlight
will disappear, surely?
There is nothing that does not disappear.
I disappeared before I was even born.

For Peonies

It hasn't been born yet, but it's already bloomed.
It hasn't bloomed yet, but it's already beautiful.
It's not beautiful yet, but it's already fragrant.
It's not fragrant yet, but from afar
a swarm of butterflies comes flying and the flowers fall.
Spring hasn't passed yet but in the whole of nature
the sorrow of joy shines bright.

The Snowman's Grave

The snowman died today.
It's as if my father had died.

Somebody came along snowy paths from far away
bringing an urn.

I carefully put the remains of the snowman into the urn.
Bones of water.
I prepared no separate grave.

A snowman doesn't need a grave.
Dazzling in the sun,
the place where he attained Nirvana is his grave.

Silence

Before an ant was sliced in half
in search of spring paths,
before a snail crushed
in search of forest paths,
before an earthworm in search of rain-soaked paths,
drying out and dying in the sun,
before a dead cicada fell to earth
with tattered wings,
unable to find the way to the sky,
all human steps pause and pay silent respect.
Until above the distant horizon
the smile of a young man on a cross
becomes a twilight glow.

I Kneel

I kneel when flowers bloom.
I kneel when showers fall.
I kneel when dead leaves go rolling away.
I kneel when the first snow falls.
I kneel in front of the snowman made from the first snow.
When the stars look down at me in the dark
I kneel.
When You tell me to kneel
I do not kneel.

A Snail

Spring rain is falling.
One old woman
with a cart full of cardboard boxes,
her bent back even more bent,
like a sluggish snail,
is slowly climbing a hillside alley
in a redevelopment area
on the outskirts of the old city
dragging an old cart.
Humbly sitting alone under the eaves
of an empty house her neighbors have left,
until the spring rain stops,
she tears apart the rain-soaked cardboard boxes
and eats them hungrily.

Raising Birds

What raises birds is a blizzard.
It's a biting wind that passes among the branches of winter trees.
It's the patience that endures the wind.
It's the crimson smile of the last persimmon
at the tip of one high branch.
It's the tears of my mother who appeared in my dreams last night.
It's the moderation that does not eat every bug,
does not fly through every sky,
does not perch on every branch.
It's the calm of cool winter moonlight.
It's thanks for the red cornelian cherry
that withstands heavy snow and calmly reveals its heart.

Stumbling Block

When did I knock anyone down?
When did I bring anyone down?
I'm nothing but a stone,
deeply rooted in the ground,
looking up at the sky,
merely the fruit of a stone with flowers blooming at its root.
When did I disturb human love?
When did I obstruct human desires?
Even the wind doesn't catch on me,
fallen leaves pass me by,
even thick snow falls quietly and settles.
I do not bring anyone down.
People trip themselves up, stumble
and simply fall.

Dreaming Dust

Dust's dream is to become soil,
to become the soil of spring or to become a barley field,
to become the soil in a flowerpot where bulbs sleep,
making a single daffodil grow up and bloom is its dream.
Even if the dust wanders the subway endlessly,
it dreams of sitting down,
settling down to a lower level,
becoming the food of the people on the subway.
Caught between the passengers on a hungry commute,
dust dreams of creating a world where dust becomes rice.

The Road to Buseoksa Temple

When a still unripe apple fell
in the apple field stretching along the road leading to Buseoksa Temple
I cried after losing yet another love.
That summer I spent as a young wanted man
in my aunt's tiny room at Buseok Inn
I tried to comfort the young apple's heart,
explaining why young apples have to fall to the ground,
why worms have to eat young apples,
by saying that insects have to live too,
even insects have to live to become insects,
and on summer nights when my aunt and I propped up apple tree branches
before we fell asleep, my aunt would hug my thin shoulders,
saying that the place eaten by insects
was the place where a hungry star had taken a bite the previous night
and that the more we live, the more wounds shine like starlight,
and in the summer apple orchard of that hot wanted man
if yet another unripe green apple fell
I would cry again, having lost your love,
who would squat crying in front of the autopsy room.

To Become an Empty Bowl

If an empty bowl exists merely as an empty bowl, it is not an empty bowl.
An empty bowl has to be filled then emptied, filled then emptied.
An empty bowl that always exists merely as an empty bowl
is neither humility nor beauty nor holiness.
In order for an empty bowl to become a truly empty bowl,
it must first know how to be full.
It has first to be full, whether with wind, clouds, or rice.
While waiting for people to eat all that filled it, growing empty again,
it has to gaze at the blue sky

If it doesn't know how to be full, it is not an empty bowl
An empty bowl that does not know how to be full
does not know how to be empty.
When you tell me always to be an empty bowl,
you are telling me first to be full, then satisfy everyone's hunger.
Since I must be full in order to be empty,
and must be empty in order to be full again,
if nothing is filled, it cannot be empty again.
Since an empty bowl that is always empty is not an empty bowl,
nowadays I go out into the cold alleys waiting to be filled.

A Salmon

If it's not the way, I won't go.
If I don't go, it won't be the way.
The reedbed by the river where you are waiting,
a young ferry floating all alone,
if it's not the way, I won't leave.
I couldn't provide a flowered bier
for my mother who died after spawning,
but I will set off for a distant continent's river
to be a mother like my mother
along a turbulent forest path
through the sound of a strong sea wind.
Since I can't wait, if I cannot bear it,
since I can't love, if I can't wait,
even if I tell hungry fish
to nibble my body's whole heart,
on the banks of the river where you wait
when the red moon rises, people sometimes come visiting,
sprinkle a handful of ashes, and return back home silently
and once I get there, I will sow tears.

Looking at a White Pine

All expectation has vanished.
I no longer need to be tamed by expectation.
Sleepless nights must also disappear.
Thinking that there was a pure expectation somewhere
was my mistake.

All hope has vanished.
I no longer need to be tamed by hope.
I do not need things such as despair.
Thinking that there was a sincere hope somewhere
was my mistake.

I do not wait for spring to come now.
Spring always came when I didn't expect it.
Winter is not there to prepare for spring,
it is there so that I can experience winter.

Even now, put down white roots on the top of a cliff.
White snowflakes should pile up carelessly at the tips of pine branches.
You never have to be shy
of the wounds of anger revealed white to the very quick.

Arirang, Even if Trampled On

I will laugh even if trampled on.
I had absolutely no idea
that tragedy was blessing turned upside down.
I will laugh even if the flowers fall.
I will laugh at the sight of flowers blooming by your grave, even if I bleed.
I will laugh, even if birds bleed as they fly.
Even if blizzards fall on snow-covered mountains and streams,
even if fresh snow falls again on a spring day with azaleas in full bloom,
I will not cry after laughing.
I will laugh even when blood flows from trees in dark streets,
laugh even when blood flows from the clouds in the night sky,
laugh even when tears of blood flow from the stars.
Until I am trampled down and become a winter barley field,
until I become a blood-stained song in a barley field,
though I be trampled on again and again,
I will sing *Arirang* alone.

Today's Resolution

I will never love you again.
If I can truly do that,
I will hate you every night and never fall asleep.

I will never pour water into a broken bowl again.
I won't crawl about, trying to drink that water.
No matter how thirsty I am,
I will break the broken bowl again.

I will never again fall alive into Hell.
I won't cry even if I fall into Hell.
No matter who holds out a hand to me in Hell,
I'll once again let go of the hand that I let go.

Even if spring comes to the cliffs of Hell
I will never rejoice or fear again.
I'll dry armfuls of the petals blooming on the cliffs,
sit alone at the edge of the cliff, and brew tea.

For the Last Time

This is the last time I shall forgive you.
This is the last time I shall love you
in the prison camp of life.
And this is the last time for me
to practice the words of Mother Teresa,
that we can be forgiven when we forgive.

As for meeting and eating stone-pot rice with dried yellow corvine,
sitting by a warm window and drinking coffee together,
taking a train to far-away Sokcho,
gazing at Mt. Seorak and shedding tears of repentance,
you growing infinitely small
as you bow to the bronze Buddha at Sinheungsa Temple

Today is the last time.
You always put off today's love until tomorrow,
but tomorrow's love won't come.
Because no one listens though you tell the truth.
Now is your chance to speak the truth
you did not speak for fear.

It's okay, even if you fail life for the last time.
Failure is rather comfortable.
It's difficult to succeed in life by loving.
In the prison camp of life
today is the last time you betray me
and I betray you.

Concerning that Loneliness

Even if you can't remember love,
anger will be remembered.
Even if you don't remember prayer,
hatred will be remembered.

Today, again the wind blows, rain falls,
and after the rain has ceased the clear sky is even lonelier.
No matter where your confessional is,
my confessional is in you.
Last night a rat gnawed away my heart,
so I cannot make my way to you.

In the meantime, every time I walked along the road,
I walked along wearing two pairs of shoes.
Whenever I ate along the road,
even after eating ten meals a day, I was hungry.
Whenever flowers bloomed, I thought that they were money
and uprooted dandelions.

Still today, I couldn't find your confessional
and the sun is setting forever.
Now is the time for me to obey the moment of separation,
unable to see flowers that bloom even without soil,
stars that shine even without a sky,
it's time for me to vanish, lonely.

To a Flock of Teal

I too have become a bird flying through the sky.
In that brilliant group dance of a flock of teal
across the river, spread over the distant winter sky
where the sun is setting, finally I'm dancing as a bird.
As I went staggering aimlessly
with the human anger that never disappears,
it allowed me to perform a dazzling group dance to my heart's content.
Even if I dance a group dance of sorrow,
since I have forsaken nothing in the meantime,
gathering and scattering, scattering and gathering again,
at every moment of the group dance, I will forsake everything.
Becoming the most beautiful bird among the humans who have
    become birds,
I will make all human beings beautiful.
Even if the flock of teal disappears in a flash into that red, darkling sky
after the end of their majestic group dance,
I will not lose the posture of a glorious bird
as I fall to the humans' ground.

At Bulguksa Temple

Going to Bulguksa Temple and not seeing Buddha Land,
I merely wandered around near Bulguksa Post Office.
White magnolia petals were falling
over the wall of the Sillajang Inn in front of the post office.
People sat by the window of the post office writing letters,
then took out their phones without sending the letters
and made phone calls to somewhere.
I wondered if they were calling Buddha Land,
so I leafed through the phone book and made a call,
but no one answered, wherever Buddha was.
The sound of birdsong could be heard
flying into the sound of the evening bell of Bulguksa Temple
and I also heard the sound of the Dabotap stone lion roaring alone,
but when I went to Bulguksa Temple I couldn't see Buddha Land,
only followed alone the shadows of people
leaving after taking a commemorative photo in front of Cheongun Bridge.

To a Wooden Fish

Now go flying away.
Previously hanging in a mountain temple,
all your flesh and bones torn by people,
now go flying over the ink-painting-like Sobaeksan ridge.
Become a fish and leave humans far away,
visit the always blue sea of enlightenment.
Your home is the sea,
a birch forest in the deep blue sea.
Although I was squatting
all that time in your empty heart,
thank you for making a little bird
fall asleep with me all my life long.
If you have a cintamani in your mouth, throw it away.
Rather throw it into the rotten heart of a man
and go flying over the horizon.
So that you don't blaze up then collapse with thirst anymore
make the dark blue sea of eternity overflow
into your empty heart.

At the Racetrack

People turn into racehorses, go galloping.
Horses become jockeys,
lash people's asses with their whips.
On the stands, horses holding betting slips smile
as they watch people turned into racehorses go speeding.
People shout that just trusting in the odds
is the best way of living.
As a human being, you shouldn't go speeding anymore.
Even if horses gallop, people should not race.
Even if there's no sign of a desert meadow anywhere,
even if the grass flattened by the wind is unable to stand up again,
you must walk quietly along beside the desert rivers.
You've been running along that long road without hooves
and in order not to go speeding on like a racehorse
you must seize the reins of your anger, leave the racetrack,
and slowly go walking along that spring road.
To avoid collapsing, unable to reach the riverside,
you must stop trying to win life's race.

Photos Taken by Someone Blind

When a blind person takes a picture,
they take no pictures of waves, only of the sea.
They take no pictures of ridges, only of mountains.
They take no pictures of leaves, only of trees.
They take no pictures of people, only of love.

When a blind person takes a picture alone,
they just laugh.
If we look at the pictures taken by blind people,
there is only a smiling landscape.

The alleys smile, the roofs smile,
the birds flying in the sky laugh, too,
the dogs in the alleys laugh, too.
Even the invisible baby Buddha
quietly appears in the alleys and smiles.

If we look at the pictures taken by blind people,
the empty sky is full,
clouds that have passed are blooming,
silent shadows are singing,
the shadows cast by the moon are warm.

A Black Mask

That's not a mouth.
It's a mouthless mouth.
If that's a mouth, it's a mouth that eats rotten food.
It's the mouth of an ox that eats other people's fodder
once it's eaten all its own.

That's not a flower of silence,
nor is it tears of silence.
It's words of silence devoid of silence.
It's the words of a grave, already buried in the ground.
It's the words of a hungry wild dog prowling around a grave.

That's not a night sky full of shining stars.
It's a darkness where dead stars sleep forever.
It's a darkness darkening human hearts,
the night of those who have lost justice and gained hatred.
It's a mask of darkness that stinks like a sewer.

Sad and Happy

It's not because flowers have bloomed early alone that spring comes.
It's not because flowers have fallen first that spring days leave for good,

It's not because a person walks alone that a new path opens.
It's not because all roads have crumbled that roads have ceased to be.

So far, it has rained wherever I went, so that the road has turned to mud.
Yet flowers bloomed in every footstep as I walked along that muddy road.

Today, the buds on the ancient plum trees at Seonamsa have burst open and gaze at me.
Birds drunk with the scent of plum blossom peck at red plum petals and gaze at me.

I love you as you gaze at me with the sad and happy eyes of a little bird.
And you, lacking a bird's gaze, love then fall asleep forever.

Sungnye-mun, Seoul's South Gate

When, for the first time, I rashly got off the train at Seoul Station as a boy,
and I wandered at the foot of the Seoul Station clock tower, not knowing where to go,
while none but the Seoul Station Square pigeons were blankly staring at me,
running like my father, arms open wide, and holding me tight . . .

When I first left Seoul Station to find my heart's hometown as a young man,
when I came back to Seoul Station, weeping, having failed to find my hometown,
when I was soaked by the rain, lost with nowhere to go,
gently coming close like my mother, and hugging me to her breast . . .

When now I am old and have nowhere to go,
when even old friends leave me and even my old wife leaves me,
and I aimlessly take the subway to Seoul Station and look up at the distant sky,
approaching, like that skinny man I meet when I go to Myeongdong Cathedral,
who pats my bowed shoulders tenderly . . .

Never abandoning me, even when life finally abandons me,
holding hands with all the poor people living in Seoul,
even when they sing Arirang,
walking the streets of Seoul at dawn as spring begins,
taking out a handkerchief and wiping away Seoul's tears without a word . . .

Part 3

An Ant

Again today
there is no need for you to weep sadly
for me, for me who have died.

Why did Mother tell me:
If you can't be human,
at least be an ant?

The backs of ants walking to the subway station
after waking up early in the morning
are more beautiful than people's backs.

Autobiography

I go crawling down a street after the rain,
crawling like a snail.
I go crawling to receive my salary,
I go crawling to reduce my mortgage interest,
I go crawling to Myeongdong Cathedral
to pray falsely without love.
I visit Jogyesa Temple,
bow to the Buddha without putting any money in the box,
then, taken aback by the sound of Buddha coughing,
I go crawling off as if running away.
I go busily crawling
across the Han River towards Gwanaksan,
intending to say I love you without really loving,
to say I forgive you without really forgiving,
to you though I don't know where you are.
Until one day
I'm squashed when you step on me.

You

Expecting a lotus to bloom in the flames,
after setting a fire of longing in my heart,

expecting the stars to move in flocks
once a flame of longing blazes in a lotus,

Expecting you to set off for the Himalayas,
riding a mule into the lotus
with a jingling bell,

Expecting you to wait for me forever,
sitting alone on top of Annapurna
reflected in the dew pooling on a lotus leaf.

My Heartless Heart

I thought I had a heart in my heart
but where has my heart gone?

Rain is falling in my heartless heart,
spring rain.

Again today, my heart, caught in spring rain,
has come seeking me again,
before I could go seeking it.

Again today, my heart has left me
before I could leave, setting off
into the spring rain

Loving for a lifetime by loving only once
like the ancient stone pagoda on the site of Jeonghyesa, in Gyeongju,

My heartless heart
stands there, caught in the rain.

When I First Held Your Hand

When I first held your hand
I was poor.

When I first held your hand and walked down the street
I was dying day by day on the street.

When I first held your hand and sang
I was flying in the wind as a handful of black ash.

When I first ate rice while holding your hand
a bowl of rice was my hungry universe

When I first held your hand and poured you a drink
before I had even filled it I was a trembling glass.

When I first held your hand and wiped away your tears
a flower also bloomed in my wounded fist.

When I first held your hand and walked beside the river
I finally started spawning with the salmon.

While Flowers Fade

I only ate rice while the flowers faded.
Panting hard,
I only earned money while the flowers faded.
I took the money I had earned and went to the bank,
then while I waited for the endless rain to stop
I postponed today's love to be tomorrow's love.
Don't blame the flowers' reasons for withering.
Now flowers with nothing but bones will soon die.
Once the flowers have died and I have cried all winter long,
even if you don't wait, please,
become spring.

To Kasyapa

Show your smile just once more.
Although I am not someone like a flower,
although I drove a nail into my mother's breast,
finally I want to see your smile.
Since my mother finally forgave me,
I want to enjoy eating your smile,
at least once before I die,
so like the kimchi stew that my mother made,
and at last become a good person too.
I don't want death with dignity.
If you smile as you stealthily visit
my funeral parlor, where I cannot offer myself in sacrifice,
I will be able to walk on air
and go climbing up.

A Trap

I thought that I had lived setting traps secretly
in every alley I walked along,
every mountain path,
but it was not so.
Not so.
I've lived my whole life caught in your trap.
Until now I have not set one trap,
or caught even one person.
Only I
was dragged off somewhere like an animal.

A Fire

There's a fire in my life.
No telling where the fire came from,
or who lit it.

Attempting alone to put out
the roaring, blazing fire,
I went running in all directions
then plunged my breast into the well.

The well catches fire,
the bucket burns,
the flames from the well set the distant mountain alight,
Naksansa Temple is on fire.

I've been chasing around all my life, trying to put out the fire,
but instead of putting it out,
I have gone leaping into the fire
like a moth.

Stumbling

I lost my footing again today.
This wasn't the place where I should tread either.
Was it the glance of a passing bird?
Luckily I didn't break an ankle.

No matter how long I wait, I go without coming,
no matter how far I go, I don't go but come,
when in love, I can only love.
Floundering all night long, leaving no footprints,
I stumbled over Jirisan Mountain.

There was no need to give directions to fate
but while trying to give directions to fate
I even lost my own direction
so how can I walk without stumbling,
arrive without falling?

Heading for an invisible mountain,
I first walked up a visible mountain
then finally fell to my death and again
walk with footless feet,
so that on snow-swept Jirisan in winter,
the sound of a *daegeum* flute being played cross-legged
alone is quiet.

A Gate Crasher

I am a gate crasher in my life.
When I'm hungry, I set the table like a mother,
when I can't get to sleep, I spread my bedding like a wife.
I thought I was sincerely invited to life
but I am an uninvited gate crasher in my life.

Even if I don't expect it, the first snow falls every year,
flowers compete to bloom along the roadsides of life.
I thought I was a valued guest in my life, but I was
just a wayfarer wandering mountain paths
looking for a place to sleep for the night.

All this time an uninvited guest gatecrashed
and my guilt, interfering with and harassing my life, is very great.
Even without being invited, I visited life,
took the offered drink like a guest,
raising and draining the cup of life's tears. Please, forgive my sin.

But sometimes birds came flying at dawn,
shat on my chest then flew away.
There were times when my life was beautiful with the scent of bird shit
so please forgive me
before gate-crashing death comes visiting.

Off the Train

Why, when I am travelling by train,
do I jump off the train?
Why, even though the train is speeding along,
am I jumping off the train and weeping?
It is not the final station.
The train doesn't stop
just because I say I'm jumping off the train.
Even if I could not make one clear hand mirror to offer you,
though grinding pebbles all my life,
or love the speeding train
while the train is speeding.
Quietly leaning my head against the window,
I gaze at the green shadows on the flooded fields
where rice seedlings have just been planted.
It's not that the train is not speeding
just because I say I'm jumping off the train.

Turn into Charcoal

Don't turn into a branch of a much-scarred tree,
instead turn into the heart of a tree on which birds come and perch.
Even if I finally set fire to the tree of treachery,
don't turn into a fire of an anger that choses the past, but instead
turn into the silent charcoal of the present that remains after all has burned.

The charcoal is the small footprints left by the stars in the night sky
with the birds that perched briefly in the breast of trees,
a black dew of the tears that birds shed all night,
for the stars to become charcoal again tonight
falls on my breast as the body of dew.

As the future lies not in revenge, but in forgiveness,
even if a forest fire of fury burns in my heart,
turn into a pile of ash wherever the forest fire passes,
finally survive in the pile of ash
and turn into a reconciling heart of charcoal.
Turn into charcoal harboring embers of forgiveness.

A Pile of Ash

How can I turn into charcoal and not just be a pile of ashes?
How can I turn into embers without turning into charcoal?
Human embers still remain in the ashes.
Some try to extinguish even the remaining embers,
scratching their way through the pile of ashes all their life long,
but within the embers are the sprouts of the topmost branches
Look at Jirisan, turned into a pile of ashes
last winter after forest fires had passed.
When spring comes, green buds sprout.

Drenched in Dew

Fortunately,
my heart is not drenched with resentment;
fortunately, it is drenched in dew.

Let not the sun set
while you still nourish wrath in your heart:
I have never forgotten your words.

But the sun never sets
and autumn comes while I still nourish wrath in my heart.
As a result, I can't even sleep
and as I walk along the road at dawn

I give thanks.
My heart is not drenched with anger,
but with dew, so I give thanks.
I am someone drenched in dew.

A Blade of Grass

The first thing I did after being born as a blade of grass
was to fall, collapse in the wind.
Falling, unable to avoid the wind's fist,
I still made every effort not to cry.
Fearing that my crying might be heard by crickets far away,
I buried my crying heart in the ground.
The poet Kim Su-yeong said that I should fall faster than the wind,
then rise again before the wind,
but I was never able to rise before the wind.
But still, as I have never forgotten you for a moment,
never betrayed you for a moment,
even if I fall in the wind, rise, then fall again,
the most joyful thing I did after being born as a blade of grass
was to turn your tears into dew,
to make the dew shine, dazzling in the moonlight.

In Order to Become Mud

I eat up all the dirt abandoned in the streets.
I drink all the water in the ditch flowing through the alley.
I secretly pick up the money people drop, and eat it.
I chew up and swallow all rotten human love.
For piles of garbage to become mud,
to become a patch of mud where lotus flowers can put down roots,
I trample myself down to make a lotus bloom
just once in a lifetime.
I trample down my heart without taking off my shoes.
Seeing the lotus blossom not stained by the dirt of the mud
I have been angry all my life and lived in rage,
asking: Why do you only bloom in the mud?
Why does the mud not stain your beauty?
But as the foulest and most trampled down mud
brings the clearest and most fragrant lotus to bloom,
in order to become the foulest mud,
today again, I trample myself down with my bare feet.

Crossing a River Alone

Once I was afraid that the river was swelling more and more.
So in order to cross the river and safely reach your house,
I waited for the river to dry up, exposing the river bed,
in order to approach you quietly,
walking on a path across the river bed.

But the river still would not dry up.
No matter how long I waited, the river bed was not a path but a river bed.
All river beds have to grow deeper to become river beds.
In order for the river bed to grow deeper
the river had to swell more and more.

Now I am not afraid, even though the river swells.
Even if the river that used to reach my ankles now reaches my chin,
even if the bottom of the river grows even deeper,
I have to cross this river alone, unable to return.
I light a lantern bright outside the window
and advance towards your house that awaits me.

Evening with Swords

I always thought that swords were soft like blades of grass in spring.
I always thought that swords were sweet like youthful lips.
I thought the day would come when all the swords in the world
would grow soft like soft tofu.
Until then, I rejoiced, praying earnestly and waiting patiently
to cook delicious soft tofu stew with soft swords,
firmly resolved to offer it to my deceased father.
But finally this evening, a sword pierced me,
making me kneel and raise both hands,
deeply pierced, in a posture of surrender,
making me realize my sin of not thinking of a sword as a sword.
I fell and bled white blood,
saying that no matter how soft a sword is, it is still a sword,
that a sword cannot gently stroke anyone's breast,
that if pierced by a sword, you have to pull the sword out quickly.
I'm not even Ichadon, but the white blood
soaks the blades of grass,
soaks the breasts of birds flying in the sky.

To the Woodpecker

Please don't peck me.
After days and days without ever sleeping,
how can I live if you peck like that?
My heart is already soaked with blood,
the wind blows in and out of my lungs,
my heart has a hole in it too, doesn't it?
Thank you for catching and eating all the bugs of my sin,
for catching and eating all the tiger moths of my lust,
but still, you don't even feel sorry for me.
Yeah yeah, okay, okay.
It's okay if you dig out all my breast,
it's okay if you reveal my heart and fall asleep there,
it's okay if my heart becomes your nest,
you love each other, lay eggs and raise young.
Although I'm a sinful human,
I'm the oak tree where you built a nest of love.
Thank you for considering me who can't be forgiven by anyone
as a strong and beautiful tree
Later, when you take your baby birds and going flying off into the
    blue sky,
don't forget to take me too.

Your Sword

In the end, living
is a matter of throwing away the sword kept in the heart for life,
and even if you take out the sword, standing on a rock,
you can't throw it away and

Even if you draw that sword and finally stab down at me,
don't stab my skinny back.
As the first snow is still falling on my back and the birds are flying,
even if you sharpen the blade like that and stab the sword down,
plunge it into my red heart.

Holding your sword in my arms until spring comes,
I go walking into the shade of a green tree,
become the heart of the tree,
and will hold the sword that all the people in the world have never
    thrown away.

If you mean to stab me with a sword,
don't stab my back where morning dew is still falling
but plunge it into my heart
where my deceased mother is still alive.

A Melancholy Officetel

The high-rise officetel shakes.
From dawn, swelling waves approach the window.
The black dawn fog also follows and sweeps over me.
It's because fate has vanished.
It's because since I left you
all my fate has collapsed like the horizon.
I was not you, and you were not me.
It was too late to start life over again.
Even if I eat rice alone in tears, my tears do not become rice.
Just as people are tricked by people in life,
it seems that birds are also tricked by birds in life.
The seabirds that came flying to the window of the officetel
with the waves take my hand,
telling me not to jump first
before the officetel jumps down from a high floor,
telling me not to cry even if fooled by hope,
they hold my black hand tight and refuse to let go.
Yes, yes, thank you, birds.
Now I'll finish where I ought to finish
and will never cry alone again.

To my Demon

Since I am so delicious,
how much do you have to eat of me to make your stomach full
after pounding me like a dried fish and tearing me to shreds?
How much more thoroughly do you have to crush my bones to make a
    satisfying smile?
Don't you have plans to cut off a trifle and grill it on the fire?
Even if there is nowhere to kneel and pray,
I've never rejected hungry love.
If you chew me, boil me, fry me this way and that, am I delicious?
Every time I take out my liver and make liquor every night,
go up to the top of Namsan Tower and raise a glass high,
my tears gathered in your cup become the Han River and flow.
Whenever the sound of glasses clashing rings in the night sky of Seoul,
my tears become bloody tears and the stars turn red.
Taking away love before even loving,
drawing a mandala all night then erasing it,
nowadays, I secretly abandon myself in the flowing water of
    Cheonggyecheon
and go home. After plum blossom falls into the Seomjin River,
plums ripen and if the ground of my love ripens beautiful this fall,
don't show rotten teeth or sharp claws,
don't smack your lips.
If you shell and eat me as if shelling crab meat.
wouldn't you feel fuller if you omit the nonsense?

To a Winter River

You should reflect now.
You have to freeze to the very heart
as soon as winter comes.
You must no longer look with autumn's eyes,
you have to grow hard like that rock rooted in a cliff.
You are a rock made of river water, a road made of ice.
Do you know how many times I've fallen in and drowned
walking over your thin ice?
A river with thin ice freezing is not a winter river.
You cry like a lion and freeze
and have to enable me to cross my winter river
as when I went to my grandmother's house across the Nakdong River
on a sled when I was a child.
I have little time left in which to cross the river.
No matter who lights a hot bonfire over your heart,
even if ice fishermen persistently hack at you with axes,
you leave one waterway for fish to come and go
and have to freeze deeper like silence.
I've always lived floundering after falling into a winter river with thin ice
and now I have to cross that winter river
where the tears of my whole life are frozen.

Part 4

Morning Star

Among the morning stars,
the clearest, brightest star
is the person I love.

Among the morning stars,
the darkest, saddest star
is the person who loves me.

Star Rice

There are many stars in the sky's well.
As my mother sat by the well washing the rice,
she said: no matter how many stones there are in rice,
they are never more numerous than the grains of rice.
She gazed at me as she spoke, child as I was,
but there were always more stars than rice in my well.
Still now, if I'm hungry,
I lower a bucket deep into the well in the sky,
pull it up full of stars, that I cook and eat.
Sometimes I mix in clouds as I cook star rice,
then set off in search of the mother I miss.

Piercing Your Heart

Piercing your heart means loving.
Loving means piercing your heart.
It means building a house like Doknakdang in Gyeongju
on the mind's cliff-edge
as the sun sets again today.
With no sunset glow, no inn across the river,
and though the morning star does not rise,
it means struggling
to cross a deep, rushing river alone.

To Love

Did you manage to walk all this way on your knees?
I was barely able to crawl here barefoot.
You became the night of a mourner who finally stopped crying,
while I eventually became a morning star that lit a lamp of tears.
You have now reached the sea and become a black horizon
while I went beyond the horizon
and became rough waves climbing the cliffs of an island.
Ah, my self who loved but hated my whole life long!
Today one seagull,
holding a wave in its mouth, disappears over the distant horizon.
Without wings I perch on the island's shore
and after laying some gull's eggs, I fall asleep forever.

Yearned-for Yearning

Were all enemies once comrades?
Was yearned-for yearning also an enemy?
A cricket stares at me and smiles,
seeing me walking about with my heart's hands handcuffed,
unable to do today what I have to do today,
unable to do tomorrow what I have to do tomorrow.
The moon's shadow caught on a persimmon tree branch sees me and
    smiles.
Outside the gate, it seems someone had come visiting,
for a black van is still standing there
and in the moonlight, several ripe persimmons fall next to some dog
    shit.
I quickly undid the handcuffs of my heart full of yearning,
cleared away the moonlight-stained dog shit.
My mother, who was eating a late supper, silently,
sets aside a spoonful as dog food.
The full moon hunbles itself,
caught in a yearning persimmon tree.

Candlelight

I placed just a single candle
on the birthday cake I had bought
for Mother's ninety-fifth birthday,
lit only that one candle.
It was not that I thought we only live once,
have one life.
Just by doing that,
Mother looked yet more beautiful.
After we sang Happy Birthday in tears
at the thought that this was Mother's last birthday,
with her expiring breath
Mother blew out the candle
then laughed sadly.
Instead of Mother, I said in my heart
that when a candle goes out it burns up again
and placed in my heart
my mother's blown-out candle.

Food

You renounced food.
You also renounced me.
Rain fell outside the window.

A thief broke into you
and I stayed up all night
to catch your thief.

While I dozed briefly
you followed the thief,
piercing the rain,
and vanished somewhere.

Like you,
a thief has entered me
so on the day I renounce food,
I will meet you again.

Mokpo Station

I shed tears when I get off the train at Mokpo Station.
Are the "Tears of Mokpo" in Lee Nan-young's song my sad tears?
When I got off the train at Mokpo Station before,
the waiting room was full of the song "Tears of Mokpo,"
that flowed like a young mother's heartbroken tears,
but now even the people of Mokpo's tears have dried up,
the song has disappeared and if you climb Mount Yudal
only a recorded song drifts from Lee Nan-young's memorial stone,
becomes a crane flying over Mokpo Bridge amidst white clouds,
goes flying to Samhakdo.
Mother,
tonight, just as you you used to sing with your long dead voice
in my childhood
please sing "Tears of Mokpo."
Your old son, who did not witness your death,
 has come to Mokpo alone today.

Now it is time to cast off
llife without Mother.
If I go to Mokpo harbor
after buying a bowl of seafood *jjambbong* at Mokpo Station,
let me hear the siren of the boat leaving this life.

A Thimble

One worn thimble
left in my deceased mother's
sewing box,
Mother's thimble
with which she used to mend the buttons on my suit,
the holes in my socks,
even used to mend my tears all my life long,
Mother's chest finally dried up.
When I walk alone at night
without knowing where I'm going,
floating high in the night sky
the lonely half moon
keeps following me.

Longed-for Lamplight

When will I ever see again,
seeping through the crack of her bedroom door,
the lamplight of Mother sewing.
When will Mother be able to don her reading glasses
and stitch up again my many wounds?

When will I be able to visit heaven again,
following the lamplight seeping through the crack of the door
of the room opposite, where Father prays
with hands joined on the Bible.

The longed-for apricot-hued light of the village
when I walked along with my mother,
the light that used to light up my room as a boy,
dispelling all fear of the world's darkness
as I fixed my eyes on it and the distant dawn.

Commemorative Photo

There was no longer any need to take a commemorative photo.
After burying my mother one spring day and
after taking a commemorative photo in front of the grave,
what remained to be commemorated?
Could despair be commemorated?
Once, when a tree was embracing me,
when an ant was walking along the road holding my hand,
we took a commemorative photo,
and we took a commemorative photo for Mother's ninetieth birthday
lighting candles as she sat in her wheelchair,
but now there is nothing to commemorate,
no life to take a photo of.

Leading my Shadow

The sun is setting
and there is a place I must go, leading my shadow.
I don't know where that place is
but Mother knows.

Mother promised to tell me
where that place is
and who I have to meet there,
but then she left in a hurry without a word.

Do I, who have betrayed my shadow all my life long,
now have to go somewhere without Mother,
leading my shadow?

As I sat on the stone steps of Seoul Station
with the shadows of the homeless,
the day I followed the sound of the trains leaving,
even my shadow left me and set off for somewhere.

The sun is setting
and will I be able to meet someone somewhere
if I become a person with no shadow?
Even if the sun were to rise tonight
I can't go to visit you.

House of Tears

I felt sad to think that night was coming and morning not coming,
so today tears bloom as flowers.
I gathered all the tears in the world that I had shed
and sowed them like flower seeds in the flower bed Mother cultivated
but not a single flower bloomed throughout my life,
only the poisonous mushrooms of hate and anger grew,
so every day I ate poisonous mushrooms and collapsed by the wellside.
Tears turned into flowers today as soon as Mother died
and became a small house of tears with a flowerbed.
Carrying the house of tears on my back like a snail,
I hurriedly set off to the place where Mother went.
Heading for the flowerbed of the House of Tears,
leaning against the wall with rose moss flowers blooming,
I become the old man of a hungry boy eating cup noodles
and set off to see Mother.

Birds' Shadows Do Not Fly

Birds' shadows do not fly.
When a bird flies across the sky
it goes flying away leaving its shadow on the ground.

Just as when Mother went back to heaven,
she went off leaving me on the ground,
so too birds go flying off leaving their shadows on the ground.

Some birds sometimes even leave birdsong behind.
At such times, the birds' shadows, eager to hear birdsong,
gather in the forest, not realizing that they are hungry.

A bird's shadow is greater than the bird.
It sends the bird flying across the sky
and never flies across the sky itself.

Inside the Word 'Whale' There Is Mother

Inside the word 'whale' there is Mother.
On Mother's hometown beach
is my first love walking along a blue path.
a sea of maternity of unknown depth,

Inside the word 'whale' there is poor Father.
There is father's blue gaze as he looks at the distant horizon,
putting down his A-frame.
There is diligent Father's earth.

Inside the word 'whale' there are stars.
There is the bright sea of the morning stars.
There is the sound of the wave-like laughter
of children running along the beach like baby whales.

Whale,
every time I close all the world's eyes and quietly
call your name,
the sea's beating heart can be heard.
The sound of my tears' beating heart can be heard.

Homecoming

I board the night train and leave Seoul Station.
When a river flows into the sea, it tastes salty,
but when I flow into the sea of Seoul I don't taste salty,
so I'm flowing back to my hometown river.
It is a sad thing to be eating ramen cooked in a pot in Seoul alone.
Getting off at my hometown station as the crescent moon sets,
it is also sad to buy and eat a double *jjajangmyeon* alone.
A few people from my hometown so full of farming,
intent on going somewhere else once again.
are blinking like the red numbers of the electronic clock
on the wall of the waiting room.
Are the flocks of teal that followed me this far
now flying far away across some night sky?
In the strong stench of homelessness in the waiting room chairs
lingers the smell of my hometown home's latrine.
Please, Mother, forgive
your son like anchovies left after brewing soup,
your elderly homeless son.

Break-Up

The branches of trees do not desert the bulbuls
because heavy snow has fallen.
The winter sky does not part with winter
because the clouds are frozen.
It's not because the stars are frozen
that your night sky doesn't shine.
After you declared a separation and left
for good because of poverty,
why do I dream hungry dreams every night and often cry?
Why do I grab and eat the bread in someone else's hands,
then cry alone in someone else's house?
If ever the branches desert the birds,
if the night sky parts with the stars,
if the rising tide on the mud flats refuses to meet the ebb tide,
if after the seedlings are planted, the paddy fields abandon the ripening rice,
if Kasyapa breaks up with Buddha forever,
how can your love ever be complete?

By the Seomjin River

If I look at the river's waves, splendid in autumn sunlight,
and think that is all there is to the river, I am wrong.

Not realizing that the river flows over the riverbed,
not realizing that fish live on the riverbed,

If I look at the river's waves dazzling in autumn sunlight,
and think that it is all the beauty the river has, I am wrong.

The reason why the fish must die, then go floating
belly upward on the riover
is because they have lived their whole life on the riverbed.

The reason why I slowly walk across the blue sky
with an empty heart when it's time for me to die

Is because after spending all my life lying asleep on the floor,
I rose from the floor and greeted the morning.

Ginkgo Leaves

Why do the yellow ginkgo leaves that started to fall from late autumn
never fall on the eaves of my heart,
but only pile up high on the roofs of cars parked overnight?

Why do the ginkgo leaves that fall more and more with the deepening
 season
never accumulate in the depths of my heart that loves you
but only follow the sound of the evening bells echoing high in the sky?

Again this autumn, the ginkgo tree at Gaesim-sa temple in Seosan
has built a beautiful latrine of ginkgo leaves,
making beautiful the hearts of all who come to relieve themselves.

I feel sad when I see the cars in the apartment complex where I live
covered with ginkgo leaves overnight.
Maybe I have more sins than a car has.

The Road along the Wall of Deoksugung

Every time I say I love you
as we walk along the road beside the stone wall of Deoksugung Palace,
I long for my mouth to become a flower bud.
And as the road beside the stone wall of Deoksugung Palace
is the sweetheart of roads, the mother of roads,
every time I say I love you as we walk together
along the road beside the stone wall of Deoksugung Palace
I long for flowers to bloom from my mouth.
My mouth being full of flower seeds,
every time I say I love you, I long for flowers to bloom,
covering the stone wall of Deoksugung Palace with bouquets.
At night, the numerous footprints left by those walking
along the road beside the stone wall of Deoksugung Palace
meet together and tell each other: I love you.

A Night in Silla

I want to spend one night with you in Silla.
Even if you really hate me,
at least once in a lifetime
I want to go walking lovingly toward Cheomseongdae,
hold hands in an alley somewhere near Bunhwangsa Temple.
Maybe the night sky of Silla
is waiting for us brightly in Banwolseong?
In order for us to fall to Cheomseongdae as shooting stars
in the sublime joy of love,
perhaps I should sleep with you
this autumn night?

Rags

After eating a bowl of *jjajangmyeon* I walk along a street.
The road I have lived on and the road I have to live on
have become rags and are hanging in the evening sky.
The stars are just starting to appear.
A bird that has been perching on the sunset
drops shit on my chest and disappears into the distance.
My shadow stretching far across the road
becomes rags too
drags me off somewhere and doesn't return.
When I walked along the road holding your hand,
my hand always shook like a blade of grass
but now all I have left is a pair of worn out shoes.
The road I have walked along and the road I should take
have become rags and been soaked with dew at night.
When starry night comes, rags are also beautiful.

Pyeongchang-dong Monastery

Only simple monks live in the Pyeongchang-dong Monastery.
They are so simple that they don't even realize that they're simple.
No matter how the birds living in the hills behind the monastery say
    they're simple,
no matter how they langh at their simplicity, chirping *simple*, *simple*,
they laugh at the mountains

Among the simple monks living in the Pyeongchang-dong
    monastery,
the simplest monk eats rain instead of rice.
When spring rain falls on Mt. Bukhansan, he thinks he's a pine tree,
holds out his arms all day long, catching raindrops to eat.
Sometimes he prays all night long, lamenting that the fish he raises
    in a bowl
eat no rice, only eat water.

Today, again, because of the Pyeongchang-dong monastery,
all Seoul becomes a monastery.
Because of the simple monks living in the Pyeongchang-dong
    monastery
the people living in Seoul don't realize how simple they are
and all become simple.
All winter long, whenever it snows, they say the first snow is falling.

In Gwanghwamun

Now is not the moment to be silent.
Silence is the moment to speak.
The sword becomes a flower, the gun becomes a fallen leaf,
cannons and missiles become ripe autumn persimmons.
Gunshots, yes, gunshots become Mother's songs,
the moment to tell the truth of silence.
Longing for Mother in a grain of rice,
I go running with a shovel and open the sluices for the waters of freedom
in the paddy field banks,
it's the moment to sow rice seeds and share makgeolli.
It's time to irrigate the rice fields and bow down to the year's harvest.
It's time to take out a bowl of love and wave a hand toward the blue sky.
When the cows fall asleep after ringing their bells and laughing,
it's the moment to overhear the frogs making love to each other,
silently in the paddy fields' night mist.
It's time to go out to Gwanghwamun carrying lanterns
and wait for the rice flowers of peace to bloom again
so that no one is sad now,
so that no one is hungry because of truth.
It's the moment for the Korean Peninsula to be covered
with the scent of rice flowers.

Boundary

There is no boundary at the border.
No one can respect borders.
Birds too don't respect borders.
Birds heedlessly cross borders.
They just fly through the sky bearing the border in their beaks.
There is not one bird like humans
who can't abolish boundaries at borders.

Part 5

Prison in Heaven

Someone is building
a prison in heaven, saying that
heaven too
needs prisons.

Today I received a text message
saying that the prison will be completed
at the time of my death.

Even if I want to cry,
trapped in heaven's prison
before you,
trapped forever,
I won't cry.

Indulgence

Even though I have no sins,
if you say you will grant an indulgence,
I will confess all my sins.

Even though I have never committed a sin,
if you say you will give me one indulgence,
unforgivable
not loving you as I am,
I will admit all my life's sins

If I fall prostrate and offer all the money from the house I sold,
and cut off all my limbs,
before I die,
even now, it's not too late.

So please, sprinkle holy water
and give me an indulgence.
Although I have committed no sins.

After Resurrection

Even after resurrection, resurrection is necessary.
Even after resurrection, you don't love me.
Withered flowers wither again,
penitent trees stop offering penitent prayers,
dried-up rivers dry up again,
dead stars start to die again,
and since I lost the truth and collapsed
even before I loved you,
even after resurrection you
must be crucified again.
In order to go beyond you to you,
even after resurrection, the dawn of resurrection
must come visiting.

Old Clothes

I throw away all my old clothes
without preparing new clothes.
All the new clothes that I gratefully washed every day
became old clothes.

The days when I tried on this and that outfit in front of the mirror
every time I went out, saying: I have a lot of clothes to wear,
all soon disappeared
and nowadays I don't even have time to prepare new clothes,
so today, I can't even share a loving glance with you
and go to Hell wearing my last cast-off old clothes.

An angel living in Hell
who came to throw away old clothes like me,
unable to even get new clothes,
stares at me,
carrying the old clothes that I discarded.

A Bus Stop

It was nice when the bus didn't come even if I waited.
After waiting in a long line with a heavy bag
for a bus that didn't come,
it was nice when I turned into a snowman and went walking
to the house where my mother was waiting for me.
It was nice to be able to become a snowy path
after sharing poor love with a lost snowman.

It was nice when the bus didn't stop at the bus stop.
Waiting in a long line while gazing at a cell phone
may not be life but
nowadays, as I queue at the bus stop,
I'm afraid the bus will soon arrive,
full of death's passengers.
The road I have to take has disappeared, the house has collapsed,
I'm afraid that you, unexpected, will suddenly come visiting.

Every Time I Look at the Clock

Every time I look at the clock
a bird flies to the window and weeps.
Don't look at the clock, look at time,
a bird's life is also made up of time.

I'm so pitiful,
not looking at the time every time I look at the clock,
that a bird comes flying to my old window
and wipes away my tears.

Realizing that since I hadn't let go of time,
time was not going to let go of me.
Time always kept faith with me
but I have never kept faith with time.

I look at the clock again.
Suddenly, it's time to leave.
A bird holding a leaf of the last hour in its beak
comes quickly flying to the window.

The Last Bus

Taking the last bus or train has became more frequent.
Whether it's a train or a highway bus,
always taking the last one, late at night,
hastily going up to Seoul where deceased mother lives,
has become more frequent.

Even if it stopped snowing on that cold winter's night,
the last train I was waiting for never came,
but now, even without waiting anymore, the last train comes.
Telling me that if I miss the last train I can never go to you,
it picks me up and keeps running along the night tracks.

If I take the last bus,
finally, I'll have to say I love you.
Eyes brimming with tears,
I have to gaze for a long time
at the beloved faces that I long to see but can never see again,
looming in the bus window I lean against.

To Time

Don't ask me what I loved.
Don't ask me who I loved.
The more I love, what more could I have to say?
I merely lived dligently until rice turned into tears.
I've already lost my way and am crying out here alone.
Even if night grows darker, the sun doesn't set,
even if morning comes, the stars don't set.
There were times when I waited alone and wept,
but don't ask me what and how I loved.
Truth also means weeping alone in silence.
Whatever I loved then lost my life,
maybe there was true love even in lies?
Please, don't ask
whether love gave birth to hate and hate gave birth to love,
whether dislike and hatred were needed and had value
in order to realize true love.
The more I love, the more I lose love,
so what way of life can I become?

The Last Moment

I'm selling my soul.
I'm selling it to the devil rather than to an angel
because I am more like the devil.
I won't make it expensive,
might even offer a discount.
You must be busy.
Thank you for having bought me,
though I couldn't live as an angel.
It'll soon be time to close the store.
Please come quickly.
I can sell my soul sliced and diced.
Even supposing I doze off as I sit at the counter,
please don't shake me and wake me up.
I'm afraid someone will wake me from deep sleep,
urging me not to look back but to cross together that strong-flowing
 stream.
I have never yet told anyone
that my sin is love, not poverty.
Even though I sold my soul, I haven't received any money yet.
I'm worried that once across the river someone will hold out a hand
and ask for that money.

In a Delta

We are each of us a river.
To reach the sea once in a lifetime
in a desolate delta in an estuary
where a river meets the sea
we go flowing after a last farewell kiss, and disappear.
Sometimes there are people who reach the sea,
but most delve into the river bed, turn into sand, and disappear.
I grab my hungry stomach and became a sandbar,
become a snipe on that sandbar,
go flying far beyond the horizon,
but to the very end the sea is invisible,
I only gaze at the wings of the red sunset caught in the reedbeds.
Only a crescent moon floating on the river sometimes reaches the sea,
becomes a full moon and returns.
Unable to reach the sea, unable to encounter the real sea,
I disappear somewhere.

When Evening Comes

Every time when I put my shoes in the shoe rack
of the soft tofu stew restaurant in the evening,
I quietly lay my body to rest
in Samsung Seoul Hospital's morgue.
After laying to rest my mortal, far too mortal body,
as I go wandering aimlessly alone, barefoot,
along remote alleyways,
the customers sitting around each table
eating with gusto bodies of soft tofu
are all mourners who came to grieve over me.
Once it grows late, finally
as I take my shoes from the shoe rack, and put them on again,
I take out my refrigerated body and put it back on.
Then, wearing those shoes, on some distant mountain road,
or rather, there being no need to go that far,
I go to the waiting room for mourners at Seoul Memorial Park
and stare numbly at the hot flames cremating me,
visible on the monitor screen.

The Fragrance of Tears

I can't leave like this, carrying poison.
In order to leave, I must release the poison.
Seeds of the poison of hatred had grown by the window of my life,
putting down roots in my heart like a zelkova tree,
so I chopped it down vigorously with an ax
but the zelkova tree grew again,
carrying the poison of death and overshadowed my window,
so in order to leave, I must now face a time of detoxification.
Every time the poison spreads all the way to my toes
and I am taken to the emergency room,
please drop your tears on my heart.
Place the scent of plum blossom blooming in hell in my eyes.
The only thing able to detoxify poison with poison
is the scent of your tears, my dear.

Poison

All my life long, I have walked with poison in my hand.
I took the subway heading toward you,
clutching a poison
that should never be thrown away or lost,

because this poison is the poison of love.
Someday, I will take it or feed it to you.
While I firmly resolved and kept the poison,
multitudes aimed their swords at my neck.

I've been busy running away all my life.
With no time, no place, no opportunity to take the poison,
one day, I hurled the poison into the Han River,
but my hand held onto the poison in my hand and didn't let go.

Today, I am taking the poison.
No matter even if it is the poison of death,
everyone is rushing towards the subway station
holding poison in their hand.

To Judas

How is it that I resemble you so much?
I thought that I resembled my father's love
but I resemble you and have become a bird of betrayal.
How can I not truly thank you?
Is it because of the comfort of your betrayal,
forgiving one who betrayed me, who loved,
forgiving me for betraying you, who trusted?
Even if spring does not come
you summon back my lost fate,
make flowers bloom again on the roadside of my destiny.
The river has dried up and all the sand of truth
has run through my fingers,
but friend Judas,
you became a human sea in the lowest place.
Since without your betrayal
all the world's love would not have been fulfilled,
today I become a bird,
forcefully spread the wings of betrayal
and fly up to the tip of the branch where you hanged yourself.

Judas' Last Testament

Now I know why morning does not come and night comes.
You exist as love while I exist as betrayal.
To see the sky, I have to abandon the air,
to see the truth, I have to abandon you.
I knew full well what you silently wanted of me.
Betrayal is simply the most perfect way for me to love you;
sometimes betrayal belongs to truth.
I am not going to say that you abandoned me for your truth to be fulfilled.
Since what is bound to happen is what eventually happens,
I simply endured my destiny to the end with honor.
Now there will be too many Judases in every life.
Everyone will speak Judas' words and wear Judas' clothes.
Every day you will be fixed to the cross, nails driven through your hands.
Still, you revere most of all those who hurt you,
and today, again, you weep for me.

Evening Meeting with Judas

Drinking with Judas one evening
by the window of a draft beer house at Chungmuro Station,
looking at the black shadow
of the darkness that quickly came crossing the road to visit us,
I decided not to meet you anymore.
People walking lovingly arm in arm
disappeared down the stairs of the subway station.
In the streets the roots of darkness put down yet deeper roots
and I thought it was time for me to part from you.
The winter wind blew a gale,
yet that was not the reason why the bell of Myeongdong Cathedral sounded frozen.
At the last supper,
I was happiest when I ate black-bean noodles with Jesus.
When Judas silently asked, 'Do you love me?'
it wasn't because I too said I had betrayed my mother.
Even if the Myeongdong Cathedral bell that sounds like tears rings out again,
it simply means that the time of the end to your love has finally come.
I only learned by taking the cup of Judas' betrayal
why a crow has called sadly at my window since spring,
and why I must walk on the stepping stones called forgiveness
in order to cross the river called life.

A Miracle

Otherwise, would Our Lady made of plaster
shed all those tears?
Otherwise, would people
call it a miracle?
Father always says
loving each other for a whole lifetime is a miracle,
for otherwise, would Our Lady made of wood
shed all those blood-stained tears?
If I so hated you,
would the roses blooming beneath Our Lady's feet wither?
If you so wanted me to die,
would Our Lady made of stone first smile,
then spend a lifetime weeping?

Before a Confessional

I always turn away before a confessional.
I become a hungry ant and my shoes
carry me before my heart into a dark alleyway.

Please wait. Even when the light of your love is on,
come in, even if the light of your forgiveness is on,
if ever I arrive before a confessional,
I always cast away the cross.

Throwing away my cross, hanging like a winter cicada,
throwing away your cross,
that has been waiting for me all my life like a father,
I squat down on the ground, laugh, then cry.

Since I have forgotten everything I have already confessed,
since I have completely forgotten the moment
when I knew what I had to to confess,
before a confessional, like a child,
I'm simply eating melted ice cream.

Guide to Confession

Whenever you visit the confessional in the crypt of Myeongdong
    Cathedral,
bring a drop of morning dew suspended on a blade of grass.
Or you can bring the sun setting on fields after the harvest is over.
It's also okay just to bring a riverbank white with hoarfrost.
Above all, on your way to visit the confessional in the crypt of
    Myeongdong Cathedral,
first stop by the bank, withdraw all your money,
and scatter it to the hungry on the streets as if sowing rice.
When the collapsed snowman stands up and picks up the money,
come bringing the snowman's tears in your empty hands.
When you quietly visit the confessional in the crypt of Myeongdong
    Cathedral,
carelessly walk along life's snowy path,
even though your footprints in the snow are unable to become a path,
come holding the hand of a sick wife or an elderly mother.
I may come as far as the confessional door,
since I'm always eternally open
for you who cannot knock on my door,
I can knock on the confessional door,
but since I am your eternal door that is already wide open
for you who can't open me and come in,
come, becoming the morning dew. Of course, you can play
with the blades of grass in the confessional.

Prayer of Haemi-eupseong Pagoda Tree

Don't forgive me.
Prevent the first snow of dazzling forgiveness from falling
on the tips of my rotten roots and knotted branches.
Hanging high in the sky with hair tied,
day after day, unable to drink a sip of water,
as you slowly burned and died,
hanging on a wire with both hands tied,
gazing up at the heaven of eternal truth,
forgiving me to the very moment you died,
with a smile as clear as a new leaf,
don't forgive me.
May no bird come flying down and perch
on my most sinful branches.
Even though I grew up eating the holy, bloody tears
that fell beneath your feet,
Even though I grew up bearing deep in my heart like a new-laid egg
your screams as you were beheaded,
I still haven't been struck by lightning,
so do not forgive me, who live as a hanging tree,
but send down all the heavy snow that has never fallen in the meantime.
Let bloom all the flowers that could never bloom .

Note: This poem is about a Catholic shrine on the West coast where many Catholics were tortured to death in the 19th century

Wounds

When I was a young man, walking along a mountain road,
I happened to glimpse a rock that made my heart sink,
for there was a deep wound in the rock.
Finding comfort for my wounds,
I used to climb the mountain vigorously.

Now that I am old, if I happen to glimpse a rock
that makes my heart sink, as I walk along a mountain path,
since there was someone in the sky who was also sad,
that rock was ever patiently accepting the tears that he shed.
Carressing my heart that was covered with scars,
I slowly descend the mountain.

Entering Nirvana

I quietly looked for a place to cry alone.
I didn't know where I should go.
A path to the sea appeared.
Sliding on a wooden board, I went out onto the mud flats,
became a cockle, and wept
until the tide came in.

I quietly sought a place in which to die alone.
Once past the path leading to the sea
a pine forest appeared.
Countless insects were crawling through the forest.
All night long, without a light,
not crying,
I followed after the insects.

So, Farewell Now

I won't wave a hand.
Don't you wave your hand, either.
I've been hanging all my whole life
on the cross you bought me.

Just looking at you makes me cry.
Just looking at you
has made me become your destiny.
I have spent my life eating the rice left over by others
but life is too short for love,
too short for anger, too.

Don't cry.
Climbing autumn mountains deeper than death,
where first frosts fall, icy winds blow,
and even if not a single chrysanthemum blooms anywhere,
as the river grows deeper, the darkness grows deeper,
and as the darkness grows deeper, parting grows deeper, too.

So, farewell now.
The hearse I'm going to ride away in today
is slowly passing beneath the shade of the cornelian cherry trees
where the berries that the birds eat all winter long are ripening red.
I don't have a grave, so please
don't weep in front of my grave.

Funeral Mass

Please, leave my funeral mass to the birds.
Since I already received the last rites from the birds,
lying in the woods while this world was suffering
though my body has already rotted,
like fallen leaves, my heart has not rotted yet,
so let the birds gather and pray for me,
then go flying off, leaving white droppings.
It would be good if sometimes a few of the forest's chipmunks
or squirrels or titmice were to come by, but
don't let any of the people I once loved come.
Since they always threw stones at me,
although I always threw flowers at them,
and I have nothing to bequeath as yet,
although it is said that when people die, they bequeath love,
so when I'm found by the birds a few months after my death
in the forests of Daemosan Mountain,
I beg you, leave my funeral mass to the birds.

Low Tide

The low tide abhored human beings.
It also hated the beacons that shone out without fail every night,
and humans' fishing boats
setting out over the horizon
dreaming of a full load,
as it went rushing far out to sea,
vowing that it would never return.
Yet still, it could not help loving you
and kept looking back, looking back
as it left the mud flats behind,
leaving long deep footprints here and there in the mud.

Transforming Our Minds, the Miracle of Poverty

by Lee Soong-won, literary critic

Ten years ago, there was a time when provocative imagination, grotesque metaphors, and strongly dichotomous poetry spread across Korea like a kind of fashion. Nowadays, such a tide has subsided, and many poems have emerged that explore the world's humanity on a very ordinary level, calmly and deeply, giving a bright prospect for the future of our poetry. It was natural to seek the path of post-lyricism by piercing beyond the old retaining walls of lyricism, but a breakthrough made at a speed close to self-destruction, far beyond the pleasure of breaking through a new type of ice wall, revealed the dangers of over-rapid transgression. Now, there is a possibility that the tactile sense of poets seeking a new path for lyricism will shift to an interest in an 'ancient future,' in which intelligence and emotion are fused. In this respect, Jeong Ho-seung's poems deserve to be presented as a pioneering example of how modern poetry, having moved far away from the general public, can still reach the general public. If lyric poetry is loved by the public and if a way of maintaining the elegance of the spirit is detected, it will play a useful role in presenting new possibilities to those who seek the path of poetry.

A poet's work contains that poet's history. The total amount of life that the poet has lived in the world, creating works so far, exerts an intangible pressure and a sense of influence. In Jeong Ho-seung's first poetry collection, "Sorrow to Joy" (Changbi 1979), it appears as the theme of the underprivileged in society, such as a blind couple, a singer, a mixed race child, a beggar boy, and a shoeshine boy. Compassion and love for them continue to this day as a major topic of his poetic creation. In "A Blind Couple Singing," he wrote about the question of how, "To love what cannot be loved / to forgive what cannot be forgiven." It is easy to love what you can love and forgive what you can forgive. What is really difficult to practice as a person is "to love what you cannot love and to forgive what you cannot forgive." This is a project that is difficult to implement even with a whole lifetime of effort.

If we examine Jeong Ho-seung's poetry more closely, we see that he has never ceased making this effort. This is a consistent theme of his poetry, which has lasted more than forty years, and is the firm and powerful DNA of his poetic creation. In some cases, he adopts the grammar of Buddhist intuition, or uses the grammar of Christian meditation, and in some cases he shows the gestures of Taoist philosophy, but his direction is always clear. His energy is concentrated in the work of loving what cannot be loved and forgiving what cannot be forgiven. He has stubbornly remained within the limits of this topic for forty years.

In order to properly read Jeong Ho-seung's poetry, it is necessary to participate in the transformation of ideas and perceptions that the poet is pursuing. There are three poems titled "Bird Droppings" in the present collection, and "bird droppings / bird shit" appears in many other places, too. Why is the poet so interested in bird shit? The poem "Bird Droppings" at the start of the collection of poetry is a short work of only seven lines:

Bird droppings got into my eyes.
For the first time in my life
I washed my eyes clean with bird droppings.
That stopped me seeing the human landscape
that I finally wanted to see
but did not need to see.
Thank you.
    —Bird Droppings

Maybe this poem was indeed inspired by the sight of bird droppings in the snow. If bird droppings get into the eyes, they can hurt the eyes, but the speaker says, "I washed my eyes clean with bird droppings." This is impossible in reality. There are many people who love cute and pretty birds, but few people love bird shit. However, the poet says that it is beautiful when birds leave their droppings on human paths, and by walking along that path, he also becomes a more beautiful human being. He suggests that the bird and he can become friends, that the bird eats his food and he pecks at the bird's feed. When you wash your eyes with bird droppings and open your eyes, the world looks new. The end, giving thanks for being kept from seeing the human landscape that he finally wanted to see but did not need to see, contains a feeling of disillusionment, a negativity toward human reality. It means that bird droppings reveal a new landscape while hiding the ugly human landscape.

The poet pursues his own sympathy with the birds, but includes a binary, confrontational consciousness, that birds are pure and humans are not. Bird shit is the medium that overcomes and resolves the binary confrontation. In short, he is expressing a new philosophy of bird shit. He is attracted to the bird droppings that ordinary people do not and cannot love as an object of love. The youthful belief that one should love what cannot be loved is transformed into bird shit. Furthermore, in another poem the poet declares, "I am your latrine." He invites anyone "any time, leave your shit on my heart and go in peace" ("Latrine"). He wants to be a latrine that accepts all the shit of other people. Can I believe this? Since this is repeated several times, we can sense that it is the poet's firm will and belief. If we absorb the first part of this collection, we may be able to imagine becoming a latrine and washing our faces with bird droppings.

In Jeong Ho-seung's poems, nature transcends the level of equality with humans and plays an active role in attracting people to its side. Ants take the lead as human companions, and birds take the lead as human mentors. Trees become caring lovers and sometimes mothers. What is interesting is that his imagination betrays the familiar common sense of everyday life, as in the case with bird shit. For example, we can readily think that dust sinks down into being soil, but it's difficult to think that dust then turns into rice. However, the poet violates familiar reasons and dreams of a situation where dust becomes rice.

Dust's dream is to become soil,
to become the soil of spring or to become a barley field,
to become the soil in a flowerpot where bulbs sleep,
making a single daffodil grow up and bloom is its dream.
Even if the dust wanders the subway endlessly,
it dreams of sitting down,
settling down to a lower level,
becoming the food of the people on the subway.
Caught between the passengers on a hungry commute,
dust dreams of creating a world where dust becomes rice.
—Dreaming Dust

Dust is something that people tend to avoid. The government is often said to be fighting fine dust. However, Jung Ho-seung's dust has a dream of becoming someone's friend. If the dust collected in the world settles and turns into soil, that is good for growing barley and daffodils. So, can the dust floating on the subway do that? The dust sinks to the lowest place and dreams of becoming rice for the people on the subway. What does it need to do to become people's rice? It goes down to the lowest point and becomes the lowest of all, something that must be trampled on by people and buried by their footsteps. When even the dust of the dust has disappeared, it will be reborn as rice.

This dream is difficult to realize in reality, just as it's impossible to clean your eyes with bird shit, or to become a latrine and receive everyone's shit. To achieve such dreams, we need to change our ideas. We have to change our ideas, with dirty bird droppings turning into something cleaner than artificial tears, and the lowest dust becoming rice that satisfies our hunger. It is only through such transformations that a path for our lives will be opened. The poet does not say that the world we live in is boring or desolate. However, the reason he continually operates a change of ideas that betrays common sense is because of the perception that our lives are so full of vulgarity and stubbornness. Disillusionment at a heartless world that does not care about the poverty of the poor may have created the following dream:

Spring rain is falling.
One old woman
with a cart full of cardboard boxes,
her bent back even more bent,
like a sluggish snail,
is slowly climbing a hillside alley
in a redevelopment area
on the outskirts of the old city
dragging an old cart.
Humbly sitting alone under the eaves
of an empty house her neighbors have left,
until the spring rain stops,
she tears apart the rain-soaked cardboard boxes
and eats them hungrily.
—A Snail

Jeong Ho-seung has written several poems with the title 'A Snail.' In them, people are seen as snails and ants in a pure and peaceful manner, even in poor and alienated conditions. Because they are fragile and pure, they are easily stepped on by others, like snails. This poem sees an old woman, who scrapes a living by collecting waste paper, as a snail. The area where she lives is a redevelopment area on the outskirts of the city, her neighbors have already moved out, the neighborhood is empty. The old woman, who has not yet left, is climbing the hill with her old cart full of cardboard boxes. She is getting soaked by spring rain, so she shelters under the eaves of an empty house to avoid the rain.

This is a scene that anyone can picture and think about. It is the last line that makes this poem into a poem by Jeong Ho-seung. He says that she "tears apart the rain-soaked cardboard boxes and eats them hungrily." If I can clean my eyes with bird droppings and welcome everyone's shit, it may be possible to open out a wet cardboard box and eat it hungrily. The poet has this unique imagination. This imagination seems to be asking us if a poor old woman at the end of her life has ever been interested in what she lives with. The idea that a wet cardboard box could be good food for an old woman who has nothing, invites us to reflect on the meaning of her life and the basis for her survival. Jeong Ho-seung's poems certainly serve to raise such reflective questions. We should seriously reflect on the implications of the miracle of poverty, when a poor old woman eats cardboard boxes.

The poem "Pyeongchang-dong Monastery" shows a similar idea. I don't know what kind of monasteries there are in Pyeongchang-dong. However, the place name is meaningless and the landscape and circumstances of the monastery are meaningful. The monks there are simple, and even if the mountain birds make fun of them, they only laugh at the mountains in the distance. The simplest of them, like the old woman before, eats rain instead of rice. When the spring rain falls, he spreads out his arms all day long as if he were a pine tree and catches raindrops to eat. He cries and prays all night long because while he is in such a situation, the fish in the fishbowl can eat only water, not rice. Such monks do not exist in reality. Daring to speak with the standards of the world, it can be said that they are dreamers who have difficulty adapting to reality. However, the poet's idea is different. Because of these monks, all Seoul becomes a monastery, and all the people of Seoul can become simple-minded fools and, conversely, pure people.

So, is it easy to become such a foolish person? Just as it is difficult to wash your eyes with bird droppings and imagine that you might become a latrine and catch everyone's shit, it is difficult to think about the situation of a stupid, simple-minded person and accept their behavior as the root of purity. To put that thought into practice, it takes practice. It also requires more than normal practice. The following poem makes us guess what stage the poet's practice has reached.

Among the morning stars,
the clearest, brightest star
is the person I love.

Among the morning stars,
the darkest, saddest star
is the person who loves me.
—Morning Star

Anyone can think that the person they love is the brightest and brightest being. However, the idea that the person who loves me is the darkest and saddest being is an idea that can only arise when you completely deny yourself. People who love people who wash their faces with bird droppings, receive other people's shit into their bodies, eat raindrops instead of rice, or tear up and eat wet cardboard boxes are inevitably dark and sad. They are alienated from the world and have chosen to become dust. They claim to be the friends of the poor. Yet they do not give up pursuing the brightest and clearest mental state. We call those who practice and pursue this kind of life "seekers." Jeong Ho-seung seeks truth by following the path of a seeker. Like a monk making a pilgrimage to a holy place, he longs for an encounter with absolute truth.

Dip the brush of truth
into the ink of mercy
and apply eye drops
to the eyes of my dark desire.
Let the light of the eye-drops shine.
I longed to look up to You
at least once before leaving
but I haven't yet managed to open my eyes.
I have lived my whole life unable to open my eyes,
let alone the eyes of my heart.
Let me apply eye drops
one last time before I die.
With the lamp of the eye drops brightly shining
I will see You at least once,

cry hard,
then go to Hell forever.
                    —Eye Drops

    This poem evokes a scene in which a monk standing at the end of his pilgrimage summarizes his wishes before leaving the world. The speaker of the poem says that he wants to look up to 'You' at least once before he dies. Eye drops serve to open the eyes and allow us to see You properly. We open our eyes, but we cannot see the reality and truth of the world. The narrator's desire is earnest as he says that if you look at yourself, there will be no regrets even if you go to hell, because he thinks that meeting You is more important than living well in the world. So who is this You? In order to say who You is, an answer will be possible only after meeting You, but I cannot say anything about You because I have not met You. In the context of the poem, this 'You' is an absolute being composed of truth and mercy, the goal of the quest that each must pursue throughout life.

    In the poem "Seeking You," likewise, we find an eagerness for the quest. Walking along the path of searching, where "I wanted to meet You but could never meet You all my life long," the speaker falls at the roadside like the pilgrims of old. The seasons change without fail, spring comes and flowers bloom, but we can never meet. The speaker becomes anxious on realizing that he will never be able to meet You, even after time passes. He lays his head on the ground and falls asleep without reaching the river where You is waiting. He has been longing for a meeting with the truth, but could not fulfill his will and now expects a pitiful end in death with his head on the ground. As such, the desire to meet You, the symbol of absolute truth, is ardent. His will is clear even in the face of the ice-cold winter river. "I've always lived floundering after falling into a winter river with thin ice and now I have to cross that winter river where the tears of my whole life are frozen." (The Winter River). The conviction and will of absolute pursuit become stronger at the end of life.

    Even after expressing such a strong will, when he reaches the scene of his death, his appearance becomes weak and humble like a bird. His desire to love what he cannot love attracts weak cockles and insects, and again works the miracle of poverty.

I quietly looked for a place to cry alone.
I didn't know where I should go.
A path to the sea appeared.
Sliding on a wooden board, I went out onto the mud flats,
became a cockle, and wept
until the tide came in.

I quietly sought a place in which to die alone.
Once past the path leading to the sea
a pine forest appeared.
Countless insects were crawling through the forest.
All night long, without a light,
not crying,
I followed after the insects.
—Entering Nirvana

At the end of life, those who seek a place to cry quietly alone and a place to die quietly alone are the poorest, those who have reached the lowest level, like dust floating in the subway. The poet is one who dreams that dust reaches the lowest place and becomes soil. This time, he dreams of a cockle in a mud flat and insects in a forest. At the bottom of the sea, at the lowest point, there is no difference between dust, cockles or insects. All of them are capable of receiving bird shit, that will wash their eyes and make their path beautiful. If you go to the end of the sea or the end of the forest, you will meet cockles and insects, but those poor and weak beings may lead to You, the absolute being. Cockles and insects which could not be found anywhere else on the road of quest and pilgrimage, may guide me and make it possible to meet You. Maybe I can only see You after I become a cockle or an insect, a snail or an ant.

In the world of the poet's imagination, when a poor old woman eats a cardboard box soaked with rain, or when dust reaches the lowest point, becomes the soil where all things grow and so becomes our rice, You will become visible. Only when we become poor in the true sense can we meet You, the absolute being. This is the miracle of poverty. In order to properly understand the miracle of poverty and to practice it as a goal, a change of direction is necessary. A change to loving what cannot be loved and forgiving what cannot be forgiven. It is only by going beyond that point that the miracle of meeting You and receiving blessings can be accomplished. That is the driving force allowing us to go beyond this boring world into a clear and bright world. If we dream of eternity, rather than staying in the limited life of this world, if we pray for a meeting with You, we have to practice the miracle of poverty by using the transformation of our minds as a driving force. As the poet sings repeatedly, in the voice of the snails, the voice of the insects, let's make that our dream.

Poet's Note, 2020

This is my thirteenth new poetry collection and my tenth in the Changbi Poetry Collection. When I published my first poetry collection, "From Sorrow to Joy," in my twenties, I really had no idea that Changbi Publishing would publish ten more poetry collections. I express my gratitude to Changbi as a son to a father.

Come to think of it, while Changbi published those ten poetry collections, I went from being in my twenties to now when I am in my seventies. I am very grateful to poetry, and to the readers for allowing me to live a life as a poet despite the long years of ordeal. In that sense, this poetry collection is also a way for me to commemorate myself as a poet, now I am seventy. Up until now, I have tried to live a valuable life as a human being through poetry, but I do not know if I have truly lived a valuable life. However, I have never lost the belief that there will be at least one person who needs my poetry and uses it as food for the soul. This collection of poems is a collection of poems written in the process of trying to understand the essence of love and suffering, two elements that can help us understand the incomprehensible mystery of being human and alive. While preparing this collection of poems, I never forgot Cardinal Kim Soo-hwan's words, "There is suffering without love, but there is no love without suffering." Although it is a legend, I also did not forget the love and suffering of Saint Denis of Paris, who walked off holding his beheaded head in both hands.

Of the 125 poems in this collection of poems, over 100 are unpublished new poems. I was so afraid that I would not be able to write any more poetry that I included all the poems I had written so far.

I dedicate this collection of poems to my deceased parents, to my wife who is my other self, and most of all to the Absolute Being, who is my 'You'.

January 2020
Jeong Ho-seung

Acknowledgments

Asymptote: "Bird Droppings 1," "Bird Droppings 2," "Bird Droppings 3," "Self-Introduction," and "A Poem Written by Birds as Footprints on the First Snow"

About the Author

Jeong Ho-seung is the most widely read and loved poet in Korea today. His poems express the joys and sorrows of life in ways that are immediately accessible to people of all ages.

Born in Hadong, South Gyeongsang Province, in 1950, Jeong Ho-seung grew up in Daegu. He graduated from the Korean Language and Literature Department of Kyung-Hee University in Seoul, where he also completed a Master's degree. He gained recognition as a poet when he won a Spring Literary Award from the *Joseon Ilbo* newspaper. In 1982, he won a similar award for a work of fiction but his literary career has been focussed on poetry.

His first published poetry collection was *Seulpeumi gippeumege* (Sorrow to joy, 1979); this was followed by *Seoului yesu* (Seoul's Jesus, 1982); then came *Saebyeok pyeonji* (Dawn letter, 1987), *Byeolteureun ttatteuthada* (Stars are warm, 1990), *Saranghadaga jugeobeoryeora* (Love, then die, 1997), *Oerounikka saramida* (Human because lonely, 1998), *Nunmuri namyeon gichareul tara* (If tears flow, take a train, 1999), *I jalbeun sigan dongan* (During this short moment, 2004), *Poong* (Embrace, 2007), *Bapgap* (Earing My Keep), 2010, and *Yeohaeng* (Journey, 2013). The present collection, *Dangsineul chajaseo* (Seeking You) was published in 2020. The storybooks for adults, *Loving* and *Lonesome Jar: Poetic Fables*, have been translated into English, German, Chinese, and Vietnamese; his poetry collections have been translated into Japanese, Spanish, Russian, Georgian, and Mongolian as well as English. The bilingual English-Korean collections are *A Letter Not Sent* and *Though flowers fall, I have never forgotten you* (Seoul Selection, 2016).

He received the Seoul City Literary Award in 1989. He has also received the Jeong Ji-yong Literary Award, the Pyeonun Literary Award, the Sanghwa Poetry Award, and the Gongcho Literary Award.

About the Translator

Brother Anthony of Taizé (An Sonjae) was born in 1942 in England. He studied Medieval and Modern Languages at Oxford University, and in 1969 he joined the Taizé Community in France. He taught English literature at Sogang University, Seoul, for nearly three decades. He is an emeritus professor of Sogang University. Since 1990, he has published more than seventy volumes of translated works by such esteemed Korean authors as Ku Sang, Ko Un, Cheon Sang-byeong, Shin Kyeong-nim, Yi Mun-yol, and Do Jong-hwan. From 2011 he was for 10 years president of the Royal Asiatic Society in Korea. He received the Korean government's Award of Merit, Jade Crown class, in October 2008 for his work in spreading knowledge of Korean literature throughout the world. In 2015, he was awarded an honorary MBE by Queen Elizabeth for his contributions to British-Korean relations.

About the Book

Seeking You was designed at Trio House Press through the collaboration of:

Brother Anthony of Taizé, Translator
Natasha Kane, Interior Designer
Joel Coggins, Cover Designer

The text is set in Adobe Caslon Pro.

About the Press

Trio House Press is an independent nonprofit press based in Minneapolis, Minnesota. We publish poetry and prose that moves, inspires, and encourages connection, empathy, and understanding, with a special emphasis on underrepresented voices and topics. To find out more about Trio House Press, please visit our website at http://www.triohousepress.org

www.ingramcontent.com/pod-product-compliance
Lightning Source LLC
Chambersburg PA
CBHW060526080526
44586CB00012B/629